MY Awesome JUNGLE BOOK

make believe ideas

WHAT IS A JUNGLE?

A jungle is a type of forest with lots of trees, plants, and animals. They can be found in hot and tropical regions.

tiger

WHERE CAN YOU FIND JUNGLES?

There are over **8 million** species on Earth and around half of those are found in **jungles.**

orangutan

toucan

Jungles are tree-mendous!

chameleon

dung beetle

JAGUAR

Jaguars are big cats with spotted fur coats. This helps them to blend in with their surroundings.

WHERE CAN YOU FIND THEM?

CENTRAL AMERICA

SOUTH AMERICA

I walk on the WILD side!

A jaguar's jaw is **powerful** enough to crack a deer's skull!

HOW BIG?

GORILLA

Gorillas are the largest apes in the world. They live in family groups of up to 30 members.

WHERE CAN YOU FIND THEM?

AFRICA

Adult male **gorillas** are called **silverbacks** because of the **silver fur** on their **backs**.

You drive me **BANANAS!**

HOW BIG?

POISON DART FROG

These tree frogs have brightly colored skin, which is extremely toxic to predators.

WHERE CAN YOU FIND THEM?

CENTRAL AMERICA

SOUTH AMERICA

Local tribes used the **frogs' venom** on the tip of their **blowgun** darts.

I'm HOPPING mad!

HOW BIG?

ANACONDA

Anacondas are the world's heaviest snake. They can weigh up to 220 lbs (100 kg) – that's nearly as heavy as a kangaroo!

Interesssssting!

WHERE CAN YOU FIND THEM?

SOUTH AMERICA

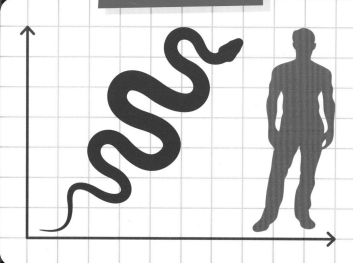

They **live** in and around swamps, **hunting** deer and **caimans**.

MACAW

These large parrots have brightly colored feathers and live in the treetops among fruits and flowers.

WHERE CAN YOU FIND THEM?

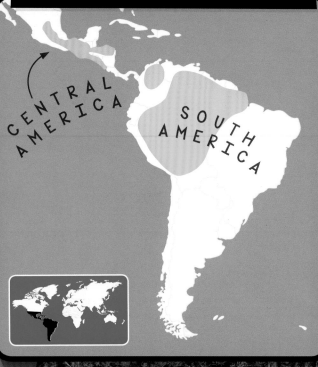

CENTRAL AMERICA

SOUTH AMERICA

BEAK-A-BOO!

A macaw has a **bone** in its **tongue** that helps it to tap **open fruit**.

ORANGUTAN

These red-haired apes use their long, strong arms to swing through the trees.

Can I SWING by?

WHERE CAN YOU FIND THEM?

BORNEO

SUMATRA

An orangutan baby copies its mother's behavior to learn how to survive.

PIRANHA

These meat-eating fish have sharp triangular teeth and live in jungle rivers.

WHERE CAN YOU FIND THEM?

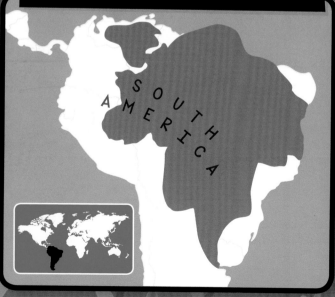

SOUTH AMERICA

HOW BIG?

I could just EAT you up!

They **swim** in groups of up to 20 to **hunt** and **scavenge** food.

TARANTULA

Tarantulas are large, hairy spiders. Instead of spinning webs, they build burrows underground.

WHERE CAN YOU FIND THEM?

I'm **HAIR**-larious!

It can **shed** its exoskeleton (a hard, protective outer layer) and even **regrow** its legs!

CAIMAN

Caimans are large, meat-eating reptiles that are closely related to alligators.

See you later, ALLIGATOR!

WHERE CAN YOU FIND THEM?

CENTRAL AMERICA

SOUTH AMERICA

A caiman has a **second** set of **eyelids** that **helps** it to see **underwater.**

HOW BIG?

SLOTH

Sloths are the world's slowest-moving mammals. They spend most of their time upside-down hanging onto branches.

WHERE CAN YOU FIND THEM?

CENTRAL AMERICA

SOUTH AMERICA

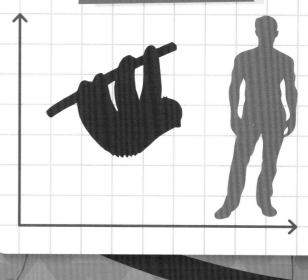

Let's **HANG** out!

They only **poop** once a **week** and always in the **same** place.

TOUCAN

These jungle birds have large, lightweight, and colorful beaks. They use them to pick fruit that is high up in the trees.

TOUCAN play at that game.

SOUTH AMERICA

They are not very good at **flying** and mostly hop from **tree** to **tree**.

HOW BIG?

TIGER

Tigers are the largest cats in the world. Each one has a unique pattern of stripes on its fur coat.

I'm not a copy-CAT!

ASIA

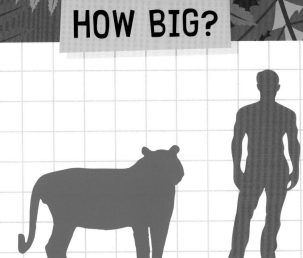

The **soft** pads on a tiger's paws allow it to **creep** up silently on its prey.

CHAMELEON

Chameleons are lizards that change the color of their skin to blend-in, attract mates, or control their temperature.

WHERE CAN YOU FIND THEM?

AFRICA

I'm one in a-CHAMELEON.

A chameleon's tongue is **sticky**, fast, and twice as **long** as its body!

HOW BIG?

INSECTS

There are more than 2.5 million species of insects in the jungle!

blue morpho butterfly

WHICH JUNGLE HAS THE MOST INSECTS?

SOUTH AMERICA

Blue morpho butterfly wings are so **bright**, they can be seen up to 3280 f (1000 m) **away!**

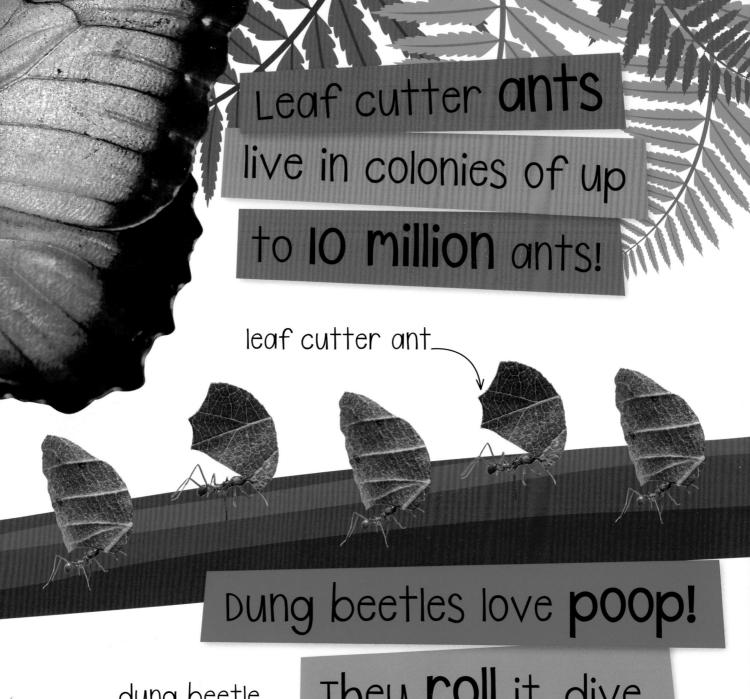

Leaf cutter **ants** live in colonies of up to **10 million** ants!

leaf cutter ant

Dung beetles love **poop!** They **roll** it, dive into it, and some even **live** with it.

dung beetle